". . . and [do] not seek
to excel
one above another,
but act for each
other's good."
—Joseph Smith

How to Make a Good Mission Great

G. Hugh Allred
Steve H. Allred

Deseret Book Company
Salt Lake City, Utah
1978

Library of Congress Cataloging in Publication Data

Allred, G. Hugh.
  How to make a good mission great.

  1. Mormons and Mormonism—Missions.
2. Evangelistic work. I. Allred, Steve H., 1952-
joint author. II. Title.
BX8661.A44   266′.9′33   78-7974
ISBN 0-87747-703-5

Contents

Learning to Love: The Challenge

*"And all work is empty save
when there is love;
and when you work with love you bind
yourself to yourself and to one another
and to God."—Gibran*

Bill lay fully awake but oblivious to the sounds of the night. Getting up from his cot, he moved slowly to a chair, passing a hand over his eyes as if to brush his confusion away. Then he reached for his scriptures. Thoughts that had been intruding on his sleep now rushed into full consciousness as he thumbed through the pages of the scriptures. "Why don't I feel right about my mission?" he wondered. "I keep telling myself everything is okay. I work hard. I'm methodical, just as I was at school. I study long hours, and yet I can't fool myself any longer. The Spirit tells me something is wrong. What is it?"

Bill had taken little time for people prior to his mission. He had taken himself much too seriously and had emphasized the tasks at school, church, and home rather than building relationships with people. As a result, he had developed much skill in getting tasks done, but little in relating to his relatives and friends in loving, respectful ways. In other words, he had become task- rather than people-oriented. He tended to be impatient and abrupt, creating bad feelings and barriers with others. And, of course, he exhibited these same behavior pat-

1

terns in the mission field in his relationships with companions, investigators, and others. Now he was finally beginning to realize, through the help of the Spirit of the Lord, that such behavior toward others is inconsistent with the gospel of Christ.

We are all much like Bill at times, for we all have behavior patterns that get in the way of our being true representatives of Christ. We can, however, learn to overcome these barriers—and for the missionary, this is most important, for the way he relates to his companions, leaders, investigators, and others determines to a large extent the degree of his success in the mission field.

Most missionaries enter missionary service with high hopes and expectations, desiring to bring as many as possible into the Church. Usually they have as their goals the attainment of deep spirituality, a strong testimony, and the ability to teach by the Spirit. They are usually willing to sacrifice in almost any way to achieve these objectives, though they may be somewhat apprehensive, because they know that many missionaries feel their missions have not been successful.

How to Make a Good Mission Great is dedicated to helping missionaries fulfill more successful missions. It suggests a foundation for all missionary work: acquiring and maintaining a Christlike way of relating to one's companions and others that will invite the Spirit of the Lord to be one's constant companion. As a missionary develops Christlike behavior in his relationships, he becomes a living testimony to investigators that the gospel of Jesus Christ has been restored and is true.

What is this foundation, this Christlike way of relating? God, through his prophets, has given the answer. The underlying focus must be righteous, loving relationships with Heavenly Father, with companions, with mission leaders, and with investigators.

This point was emphasized by Christ in his response to the lawyer's question about which was the greatest commandment: "Jesus said unto him, Thou shalt love the Lord thy God with all thy heart, and with all thy soul, and with all thy mind. This is the first and great commandment. And the second is like unto it, Thou shalt love thy neighbour as thyself. On these two commandments hang all the law and the prophets." (Matthew 22:37-40.)

Paul's epistle to the Romans (13:9-10) and his epistle to the Galatians (5:14) emphasize the same idea.

Christ taught his disciples to testify to the people that true witnesses of the Lord are known by their good fruits. (Moroni 7:3-5; Matthew 7:15-20.) And we find in John 13:35 the following message by the Savior: "By this shall all men know that ye are my disciples, if ye have love one to another."

These scriptures clearly teach us that the true missionary of the gospel of Christ will be known by the righteous, loving manner in which he relates to his fellowman and to his God. One who relates righteously and lovingly to his fellowman is able to draw the Lord's Spirit near to prompt him and help him succeed. We know from the histories of such men as Joseph Smith, who on one occasion quarreled with his wife and lost the Spirit of the Lord for a season, and from the scriptures (D&C 121:37, for example) that righteous relationships with one's fellowman are a prerequisite to having the Spirit of

3

the Lord. The missionary who earnestly seeks for the Lord's companionship will work to have righteous, loving relationships with his companions, leaders, and investigators, making this the center of all his missionary activities.

We live in a world that makes many and continuing demands on our time and energy, and the mission field is part of this world. It is easy, therefore, for a missionary to waste effort on inconsequential tasks and activities that have little bearing on his effectiveness as a missionary. Each person needs to use his limited time and energy wisely in order to become more Christlike. A missionary can direct his thoughts and actions to accomplish this by answering the question, "What should be the major focus of my missionary efforts?" The answer should become his guide, his "iron rod" in his missionary labors.

Striving for a Christlike manner of relating to others is essentially the same as striving for effectiveness in any other endeavor. God has left much of the how-to up to us. Many of us would—and do—ask our Father in heaven to tell us exactly what to do, even to the utmost detail. Out of respect for our free agency and individuality, however, he has left a good deal for us to decide. He has given us gospel principles to guide us as we search for our own answers, but much of our growth results from working out the how-to of salvation ourselves as we seek to acquire all knowledge (D&C 88:78-79, 118) with the help of the Holy Ghost. (John 14:26.)

We can liken our situation to a journey by a boat over treacherous water. God has given each of us his own boat, the gospel of Jesus Christ, and has

4

also supplied us with a rudder, the promptings of the Holy Ghost. The dangerous journey we must make is our trip through mortality, and part of this trip is missionary service. God has provided us with the essentials (for example, gospel principles) for a safe journey, but we must learn to take an active part in order to captain the boat (work out our own salvation) and to use the rudder (listen to the promptings of the Holy Ghost). Just as a rudderless boat may wander, so also we may wander when we fail to follow the promptings of the Spirit. And just as we must learn to control the course of our boat by corrections with the rudder, so also must we learn to maintain the directions of our missionary life through constant corrections (repentance). Through these corrections we can keep on a straight, efficient course for our home port, a successful mission, and eventually the celestial kingdom. Our challenge is to grow in our righteous, loving relationships with others by using the rudder (listening to the Holy Ghost) to guide us as we attempt to become more Christlike and therefore more qualified in our missionary service. Then we will find ourselves growing in those qualities described in D&C 4 that are required of anyone embarking in the service of God.

We have identified righteous, loving relationships with others as a major focus for the effective missionary. We all have feet of clay, however, and are not yet perfect in our ability to live righteously with others. The important things are that we progress and grow in our relationships, that we have the courage to recognize our imperfections, and that we have the faith and hope in Christ and ourselves that enable us to put forth the effort

5

and time necessary to progress.

This book is dedicated to giving missionaries specific guides on how to grow efficiently and speedily in their ability to develop loving relationships with their companions and others and, thereby, reap the blessings of a close-working relationship with Heavenly Father. Through prayer, he will help each one apply righteously the knowledge needed to achieve a more successful mission.

Taking Your
Personal Baggage

"We have met the enemy
and the enemy is us."
—Walt Kelly, "Pogo"

"It seems the greatest difficulty I have in missionary work is getting along with my companions. Many times when we discuss a topic, we end up quarreling, and a contentious spirit stays with us for a day or so after. Sometimes we even quarrel when we are with our investigators. Sometimes it's subtle, and other times it's very open. Though I don't like this, it continues to happen. I have prayed about it, but praying doesn't seem to prevent or even minimize this difficulty I have with others. I don't know what to do to change. What is my problem?"

This situation described by a missionary is not unusual. We have known many missionaries who have tried to decrease such difficulties by relying on prayer alone, but who have found that this is not sufficient. The Lord expects us to pray *and work* effectively and efficiently to achieve those things we desire, and the missionary who is striving to diminish contention and increase harmony in his relationships with others is no exception. If he sincerely desires to improve his relationships with others, he will both pray *and* work to discover his part in them.

Much of the tension between companions is caused by faulty ideas of how they must act in order to be important in the mission field. These faulty ideas can have a destructive impact not only on relationships with companions, but also on relationships with investigators, mission leaders, and even our Heavenly Father.

One effective way a missionary can gain a greater understanding of himself is to look at and evaluate his family and home. What is the general atmosphere of the family—mostly cooperative and secure? competitive? insecure? Where does he fall in order of birth—eldest? youngest? in between? What is the make-up of the family—all girls? all boys? one boy in a family of girls, or the reverse? one child? several children? one parent? Each of these factors tends to influence an individual's ideas and behavior, which in turn can affect his relationships with others. Each factor—family atmosphere, makeup, and order of birth—has its assets as well as liabilities. Let's look at some of them and see how they might influence behavior.

The Eldest Child

An asset of the eldest child is that it is often easy for him to be obedient to the rules and authority of the mission. He also tends to show genuine concern for others and to be responsible and dependable in his work. He may show a healthy evaluative attitude toward new ways of doing missionary work. He is often intelligent, articulate, a high achiever.

By contrast, an eldest child may use rules and authority to dominate others, and his missionary efforts may suffer as he tries to boss, smother, or act superior to his companions and others. He may use anger or a powerful tone of voice to try to get his own way. Perhaps he is overly critical of others. He may also tend to be too responsible for and too protective of his companions and investigators, to move in and do for them those things they should be doing for themselves, thus robbing them of their self-reliance. When things go wrong, he may feel that it is his fault and that he will be blamed for the irresponsible actions of others. (Parents contribute to the development of these faulty attitudes and behaviors when they leave the eldest child in charge of younger brothers and sisters and then blame him for their misbehavior.) He may also be too rigid and cautious and therefore afraid to follow spontaneously the promptings of the Spirit.

The eldest child also tends to be intolerant and critical of himself and others, and to set such high expectations that he is easily discouraged. A firstborn tends to be achievement-oriented if he is the focus of his parents' aspirations. He may equate his worth with his achievement to an extreme degree, so that when he experiences the slightest difficulty, he feels worthless and unloved. It is all or nothing for him. Such a discouraged individual may completely withdraw.

What we are suggesting is that the eldest child may deceive himself with the faulty ideas that he can be worthwhile and important only by bossing, dominating, and acting superior to others. The eldest child who is in tune with his Heavenly Father, however, tends to strive to achieve worthwhile and significant goals in the mission field through the wise and sensitive use of his special qualities of responsibility, dependability, respect

9

for rules and authority, caution, and efforts to help others.

The Second Child

A strength of the second child who is close to his Heavenly Father is that he may strive to feel worthwhile and important by doing things differently. He tends to search for new, different, more effective, and more efficient ways to accomplish the objectives of missionary work. For example, he may, with his leaders' permission, develop better methods for introducing the gospel to others. He tends to be creative, active, and to work for progress through effective change.

The second child may have, as a liability, a rebellious attitude, which is demonstrated by attempts to undermine the rules and authority of the mission. (This faulty behavior stems from resentment at being dominated by an eldest child and then generalizing this resentment to anyone in authority.) He may deceive himself into thinking that the way to be important is to be against everything, to rebel, to get people to pay attention to him. He may also play the role of a martyr in blaming others, especially those in authority, and criticizing the rules as being unfair to him, as he manipulates, often subtly, for sympathy.

The Youngest Child

The youngest child in a family is often charming, warm, and friendly. He tends to be easygoing, for he is not afraid of making mistakes, having observed his older brothers and sisters making many mistakes. He is usually tolerant of himself and others. Investigators enjoy being with him because they feel secure with him.

A liability of the youngest child is that he may deceive himself into believing he can be important by manipulating others to do things for him that he should do for himself. He accomplishes this through his efforts to appear helpless, irresponsible, and undependable. He may, for example, manipulate his companions to get him up in the morning, make his bed, and cook his meals. The youngest child in a family is often pampered and spoiled, and he may attempt to get his own way by throwing temper tantrums, yelling, screaming, crying, and whining.

While he may appear helpless, there are often times when the youngest child is actually very powerful, such as when his resentment at being treated as the smallest and youngest causes him to fight against others to diminish his feelings of inferiority. When he takes this behavior into his mission, he may do such things as belittle the accomplishments of other missionaries, parade his own accomplishments, and create artificial crises for which he presents his own ready-made solutions. He may be especially destructive when he uses his charm to keep others from confronting him with his irresponsible actions. He may also be adept at making others feel guilty and wrong, again avoiding confrontations, and getting his own way.

The Only Child

The strengths of the missionary who is an only child are often similar to those identified for the eldest child. He may be self-reliant, articulate, and highly competent and thus work well on his own. As a result he may be successful in most things he attempts.

11

On the other hand, the only child is often pampered, indulged, and overcautioned by worried parents. Therefore, he may exhibit unrealistic pessimism, timidity, and low self-esteem in the mission field. Relating to companions might be difficult for him because of his lack of relationship experiences with brothers and sisters when he was growing up. He may appear cold and aloof to his companions and investigators and may actually avoid contact with them. He may deceive himself with such ideas as "The way to be important and to protect my self-esteem is to put distance between myself and others."

The Only Boy in a Family of Girls

The only boy in a family of girls may have as one of his assets a keen understanding and knowledge of girls and an ability to relate to them in easy, comfortable, and interesting ways. He should do well with female investigators.

A liability of an only boy in a family of girls is that he may have spent all of his life struggling to achieve a male identity. He may feel threatened when he gets too close to female investigators or sister missionaries. He may, therefore, use subtle methods to belittle and put them down. On the other hand, he may feel comfortable only around women. This often happens when he has several older sisters and his father has not established a close relationship with him. This missionary may feel uncomfortable and insecure around male companions and investigators, and may unconsciously search for opportunities to be with women instead of men.

12

The Only Girl in a Family of Boys

A strength of an only girl in a family of boys is that she often has a deep understanding of males and relates to them easily and comfortably. This can be a definite advantage if she uses her understanding and skills to increase her effectiveness as a missionary with male investigators.

A liability of an only girl in a family of boys is that she may feel unsure of how to relate to women and have difficulty relating to her missionary companions and female investigators. She may exhibit helplessness and dependence, or, as is more often the case, masculine, tomboyish behavior. She may also be rather aggressive.

Missionaries from All-Girl or All-Boy Families

The sister missionary from an all-girl family tends to have as one of her assets a high degree of femininity and a deep understanding of women. These traits can be used to the mission's advantage when she relates more effectively with her female companions and investigators.

On the liability side, she may view elders and male investigators as strangers to be avoided, because she feels unsure of herself around them. Often she has had very little experience in relating to men, and she will, therefore, lack knowledge, understanding, and skill in interacting with them. One of the dangers of this is that the sister may have learned to compensate for her insecure feelings toward men by acting superior to and belittling them. She may refer to elders in general as in-

13

competent, producing conflict with the elders, who will resist her superior, critical attitude.

The elder from an all-boy family tends to have a similar difficulty to that of the sister from an all-girl family, in that he may feel unsure of himself around the sisters and female investigators. He will, however, tend to relate more easily with his companions and male investigators.

Special Conditions

Foster children and handicapped children bring quite similar qualities to the mission field.

An advantage of the handicapped or foster child is that often he has developed much courage as he has worked to overcome his problems. The foster child who has successfully learned to cope with several different families and the handicapped child who has successfully learned to overcome his handicap are often towers of courage and add great strength to their mission fields.

A liability is that the foster child and the handicapped child may have learned to manipulate the sympathies of people to their own and others' disadvantage. They may have been spoiled and pampered, and learned to get their own way and to be important by using such tactics as tears, anger, threats, and helplessness. If such behavior has become habitual, the individual will tend to use it in the mission field against his leaders, companions, and investigators.

Family Size

An individual's position in his family may also be affected by the size of the family. For example, in a family of six children who are close in age, the first, third, and fifth children tend to be similar in their thinking and behavior, while the second, fourth, and sometimes the sixth (depending on how much he is pampered and spoiled) tend to be similar to one another and quite different from the other three.

Family size and position are only two of the considerations one must keep in mind, however, as he attempts to understand his own ideas and beliefs about how to relate to others. Not all birth-order combinations or special conditions in families can be discussed in a book of this length, because the possibilities are innumerable. We hope, however, that we provide enough information to help you better understand yourself and others.

Companions and Birth-Order Combinations

In the mission field, missionaries usually spend several months at a time with one companion, getting up together, eating together, praying together, teaching together, studying together, playing together, and shopping together. Only in their future families will they have such continuing and close contact with another person. Such closeness provides limitless opportunities for developing harmony, peace, and deep spirituality, or, by contrast, quarreling, contention, and bad feelings.

Certain birth-order combinations of missionary companions tend to produce special kinds of problems. Awareness of these problems can help one identify them when they occur, which is the first big step toward reducing them.

Probably the most challenging relationship occurs when a rather typical eldest child is assigned a

15

companion who is also a typical eldest child. When two eldest children come together, there is a tendency for them to struggle against one another to see who is going to be boss, for they are both used to dominating the relationship. (This is true in marriage as well as the mission field.) They typically struggle against each other without ever really knowing why. Of course, if they understood the purpose of their struggle, it would be easier for them to change.

A bossy individual will often develop harmonious relations with a companion who is somewhat dependent, provided the dependent person is not extreme in his helplessness. When he is extreme, the dominant one tends to become too critical, bossy, and domineering, creating excessive conflict between them and more rebellious behavior (such as sulking, crying, or avoiding work or time schedules) on the part of the dependent companion.

A liability of two typical second children working together as missionary companions is that they may support and encourage one another's rebellious tendencies. An asset, however, is that companions who are both middle-born have a good chance for building a successful, peaceful relationship. They grew up with older and younger siblings and have often learned to be sensitive, diplomatic, and compromising. A typical eldest child, by contrast, tends to have difficulty compromising, believing that he will lose self-importance if he does so. His background of telling younger brothers and sisters what to do gives him little experience in the art of compromise.

16   Two youngest children serving together as com-

panions will often have special difficulties. If they are typical youngest children, each may try to outshuffle the other to avoid taking the initiative and leadership roles necessary in missionary work. Since they are often used to having others tell them what to do, they may avoid asserting themselves. Of course, a youngest child who responds in healthy ways may become an outstanding missionary; he will work extra hard to assert himself as he attempts to escape from the inferior role in which older brothers and sisters unknowingly tried to place him.

What we have discussed to this point should be considered as general guides to understanding oneself and others, and should be applied to specific cases with flexibility, common sense, and caution. No two individuals are exactly alike; no two families have exactly the same conditions for the rearing of children; and no two individuals respond to their environment in exactly the same way. When a person understands himself better, he can use this understanding to model righteousness in his relationships with others, draw the Holy Ghost close to him, and become a more successful missionary.

Seeking Help

Once a person has determined some of his own weaknesses and problems, he can begin to improve himself by seeking help from others. For example, if a person tends to be bossy, he might say to his companion, "Jim, I tend to be a bit bossy and to move in on people, doing for them what they should be doing for themselves, and undermining their self-reliance. I am working to change this be-

17

havior in myself, but it's such an ingrained habit that sometimes I do it without realizing it. If you find me trying to dominate you and to take over, would you help me by telling me about it?"

A rebellious person might discuss his difficulties with his companion by saying, "All my life I have been critical of authority figures, rules, and established ways of doing things. I guess I found a place in my family with such behavior, because I could sure shock my parents when I was critical. Maybe I learned to be special to them in this way. I am trying to change now, but it is difficult. Please tell me when you think I am being unreasonably critical of mission leaders, rules, or ways of doing things. My critical behavior is so habitual, sometimes I don't know I'm acting this way, and your feedback will really help me."

A spoiled person who is working to change his behavior might say to his companions, "My family tended to spoil me. They did many things for me that I should have done for myself. I also learned to avoid responsibility for my own poor behavior by sulking or turning on the charm. I am now trying to change such behavior in myself. It would really help me if you would tell me when you find me trying to get my own way by sulking or charming you or by blaming others for what is really my own responsibility. This behavior is so much a part of me that sometimes I don't know when I'm doing it. Your feedback will help me recognize and stop it."

It is difficult to change lifelong habits quickly. It takes courage, persistence, efficient methods, and the help of our Heavenly Father if we are to progress rapidly and solidly in developing righteous relationships with others. We may not like some of the things we learn about ourselves; some of them may even be shattering to us. It is important to recognize our problems and not retreat from them—to have the courage to face ourselves and improve. Each person has many assets to bring to missionary service; the task is to make the most of these assets and de-emphasize the liabilities. Through our efforts to improve, we can become more effective examples for investigators and new members, for personal development is a basic principle of the gospel of Christ.

Retreating from Babylon

*"Death and life are in the power
of the tongue: and they that love it
shall eat the fruit thereof."*
—Proverbs 18:21

Babylon, the ancient worldly city of Nebuchadnezzar, has become a symbol of all that is evil in the world. (Revelation 17:5.) In this chapter we use the term *Babylon* to identify worldly behavior of missionaries (as well as others) that pushes them away from their Heavenly Father and from being true representatives of Christ.

Each of us has probably been reared in a family situation in which we have learned some righteous ways of relating to our fellowman, but we have also probably learned some ways that are unrighteous. To the degree to which we involve ourselves in unrighteous kinds of relationships with our companions and others in the mission field, we will experience difficulty in more fully achieving our mission objectives.

The missionary who behaves like a man of Babylon tends to move against or away from his companions, leaders, and investigators. His general approach to relationships is a competitive one. He believes that in order for him to be important in the mission field, he must appear superior to others. His goals are often prominence, position, prestige, and power, four typical goals of the man of Babylon.

21

His desire, then, is not so much to be good as it is to appear better than his companions and others. He feels he must climb up and over others, push, and compete, as well as demean the accomplishments of others in order to make his own appear greater. He plays a game of one-upmanship in his attempts to top others' accomplishments with his own. A missionary may be so pushed against and trodden on by others in such Babylon relationships that he becomes discouraged and gives up trying to have a successful mission.

Another characteristic of the missionary caught up in the relationships of Babylon is dishonesty. He is the one who puts himself under so much pressure to appear better than others that he falsifies reports to his leaders. He may even distort information regarding other missionaries in order to make their efforts appear less important than his own.

The man of Babylon tends to be greedy. He is never satisfied with how much recognition he receives, and is always seeking more evidence of his supposed importance. It is almost impossible to satisfy this individual's greed.

The man of Babylon tends to be intolerant, negative, and destructive in his criticism of others. He focuses on mistakes and errors, allowing them to crowd out positive acts.

The man of Babylon often, in a subtle and destructive way, measures his own effectiveness against what he perceives as the effectiveness of others. An example of this is the missionary who mentally belittles his own accomplishments when he discovers that his brother in a different mission field has baptized twenty persons while he has baptized only one. Such perception is distorted and

22

gives the missionary a false impression of his own degree of success. Success in the mission field cannot be measured by the number of converts. The missionary who has baptized only one person may have worked just as hard as the one who has baptized twenty, and may have had the Spirit with him to just as great a degree, but because the people in his area generally were not prepared to receive the gospel, he found only one who was ready. His brother, on the other hand, may have been assigned to an area where the people were spiritually receptive to the message of the gospel and ready to be baptized.

Measuring one's success against the perceived success of others can tear down and destroy progress and spirituality. If a missionary starts out strong and ahead of others, he may deceive himself into believing all is well, and thus not work as hard as he should. Or if he is behind at the start, he may decide he cannot catch up with others, so he will work halfheartedly or even give up. He may feel so threatened by the progress of others that his main objective becomes that of putting obstacles in their paths to detract from their success.

A man of Babylon may also be characterized by the "yo-yo" syndrome—up one minute and down the next. At one moment he may be higher than other missionaries; at the next he may perceive his companions as climbing up and over him, pushing down on him as they surge upward. There is no secure, safe place for those caught in such relationships; every other person is a potential enemy. Relationships of Babylon are diametrically opposed to those that are righteous, and are bound to interfere with a mission. They bear bitter fruit.

23

A man of Babylon may tend to do all of the things we have discussed, depending on the people involved, the situation, the time, and the place. It takes great courage to resist becoming entrapped by such faulty ways of relating to others, for the world, which is of Babylon, tends to pit brother against brother in nearly all activities.

The consequences to missionaries who allow themselves to be caught up in Babylon relationships are predictable. They tend to belittle themselves and/or others; to fear others and suspect others' motives; to be filled with tension and anxiety; to feel grossly deficient and inadequate. They may even have opposite feelings, viewing themselves as better than others and too righteous to be bothered with the meek and the humble.

Those who are enmeshed in such behavioral patterns are often unable to cooperate with others in loving, growth-producing, spiritually uplifting ways. They tend to stimulate divisiveness, pitting individuals or groups against one another. They are often characterized by psychomatic illnesses, such as headaches, neckaches, chronic fatigue, depression, stomach and heart problems, sometimes leading to mental illness.

The final consequence for the missionary who chooses to enmesh himself with others in Babylon relationships is a degree of spiritual death. He separates himself not only from the love of his fellowmen, but also from his Heavenly Father. For a clear understanding of the characteristics and consequences of Babylon relationships, we recommend the following scriptures: Alma 4:6-15, 5:28-41, 5:53-55, 28:13; 3 Nephi 6:10-16, 11:28-30; 4

Nephi 24-26; D&C 49:20, 101:6, 105:2-5, 121:34-39.

Pinpointing Babylon Communication

All relationships in the mission field involve communication and interaction. There really is no such thing as a missionary not communicating, not interacting with others. In fact, a missionary and his companion continually influence one another and others through their communication; there is no way for them not to do so.

One of the best ways to improve communication with others and thus improve relationships is to identify those actions and behavioral patterns that are destructive and get rid of them, and to identify those that are righteous and increase or magnify them.

Let's look at four different types of Babylon communication problems, to help us better understand what we're talking about: (1) seeking attention; (2) bossing or punishing; (3) creating or maintaining distance; and (4) surrendering.

Seeking Attention

This missionary who seeks attention, consciously or unconsciously, usually expends great effort in trying to get others to pay attention to him. He out-talks others; interrupts in a nonpunishing manner; monopolizes conversations; talks with few or no questions or pauses to help him determine if others understand him—or if he understands them. Or he parades his own accomplishments before others; is too sweetly charming and flattering; asks for special favors and undue service from others; or drops names.

The following dialogue between two missionaries contains several attention-seeking examples.

Elder Jones: I'm really looking forward to our basketball game with the district leaders next Monday, aren't you?

Elder Smith: Yes, I really enjoy basketball. I played all through high school, of course.

Jones: Oh, did you?

Smith: Varsity. You bet.

Jones: Really?

Smith: First string, even when I was a sophomore.

Jones: You were varsity?

Smith: Sure, I played forward.

Jones: I didn't know that.

Smith: You bet.

Jones: I really like to play too. I think I'm going to have to get a new pair of shoes before next week's game. My old ones have just about had it.

Smith: What kind do you have?

Jones: Oh, (gives the brand name).

Smith: Well, that's the problem. That brand is terrible. They wear out. They're good for, oh, maybe three or four games, but after that you'll notice they'll start slipping around. If you had played as much as I have, you'd know . . .

Jones: Is that right?

Smith: Yeah, they're not good. You ought to go with the kind of shoes I wear.

Jones: I don't think there's that much difference.

Smith: You bet there is. If you've seen interviews of any of the championship basketball players, you know they all wear the brand I wear.

Jones: I didn't know that. Well, you know, I haven't really played that much ball.

Smith: Did I tell you about the last game I played?

Jones: No.

Smith: I made 31 points that game.

Jones: You made 31?

Smith: I was really hot that night, let me tell you. I had a girl friend in the stand—that probably was what did it. The lowest game I ever had was 17 points. Most of them were above 25.

Jones: Is that the girl you told me about who was Homecoming Queen that year?

Smith: You bet. Homecoming Queen. And the year before that she placed third in the whole state on one of her national achievement tests.

Jones: Is that right?

Smith: You bet. I only go out with the best.

Jones: I guess—

Smith: Well, those things carry over. I mean, look how many baptisms I've had. It's basically a competitive attitude that I have, Elder.

Jones: Oh, I see.

What kind of response do we have to someone like Elder Smith—boredom and irritation? These are typical responses to a person who sets a pattern of seeking attention. In this case, Elder Smith sought attention by parading his own accomplishments before his companion.

Additional verbal ways of communication a missionary might use to get the attention of others might include these: "Look at all the discussions I've had!" "I was the only one who did very well in study class—did you notice?" "Elder, shine my shoes for me. I'm working on this discussion."

Nonverbal ways of communicating a missionary might use to get attention include dressing in clothes that attract attention; continually parading his accomplishments before others; entering church and other meetings late; keeping others waiting unnecessarily.

The Missionary
Who Bosses or Punishes

Using force and coercion in order to get his own way is characteristic of the missionary who bosses or punishes. Identifying features of his communication with others might include lecturing, giving orders, talking down to his companion or investigators, correcting others, making statements or asking questions that are intrusive or probing, showing hostility or anger, whining or crying, complaining habitually about physical ailments, belittling others, faultfinding, blaming others, and making ridiculing or sarcastic comments. This person will often unrighteously justify his authority or position in order to pressure others to bend to his will.

The first episode that follows involves a number of bossing behaviors. We can better understand and identify the offensive behavioral problems if we think about our feelings about what is said rather than who says what.

Elder Jones: Elder Smith! Get in here! We're going to have study class right now.

Elder Smith: I've got a . . . My bike isn't working quite right. The tenth speed on it isn't derailing quite right. I think I'd better take a few minutes and fix it up before we go teaching. Besides, it needs to be oiled.

Jones: Forget it for now and come in for study class. We can walk this morning if your bike isn't working.

Smith: Look, I can't be walking all over town. I just had this knee operation. You know I can't handle all that walking. It won't take me long to fix the bike.

Jones: Get in here now for study class so we can get out and teach for a while.

Smith: I don't see what's the big deal. This bicycle isn't going to take me long to fix, and besides, I don't see what's so important about one study class right now.

Jones: Listen, you know the president told us we had to study. This comes from the General Authorities, who are inspired by the Lord. If you don't study, you're not following the things he has asked us to do.

Smith: I'm not against studying.

Jones: You get in here and study right now.

Smith: I'm going to fix my bike. I'll be done in about twenty minutes.

Jones: Elder! Get in here right now!

In this next dialogue between the two missionaries, note the focus on punishing behaviors.

Smith: Man, it's good to get home after a day like this.

Jones: I see you left our apartment in a mess.

Smith: Yeah, it is kind of messy.

Jones: Yeah. The thing that really bugs me is that you never pick up your socks. When we open the door, the first thing I see is those dirty socks.

29

Smith: Oh, come on. I suppose you don't leave your coat on the sofa.

Jones: I hang it up. If you want to find out if what I say is really true or not, go over there and see if your socks aren't under the sofa.

Smith: Hey, man, I take as good care of my clothes as you do yours.

Jones: Come on, you're the sloppiest companion I've had.

Smith: Well, you leave your coat out.

Jones: Ah, you're just like Elder Brown only you're worse.

Smith: I don't know, Jones. If you'd keep your coat picked up—

Jones: But we're not talking about me today. We're talking about you.

Smith: Don't be so petty. You're making a mountain out of a molehill.

Jones: You're the one who's petty.

Smith: Don't be stupid.

Jones: I'm going out on the porch until you grow up.

To the degree to which we identify with one of the participants, we probably find ourselves getting angry and feeling hurt. These are feelings that tend to parallel such Babylon communication.

Examples of verbal communication that characterizes the missionary who bosses or punishes include these: "Stop acting like a baby." "You couldn't learn those scriptures if you stayed up all night." "Why are you always so dense?" "Because you didn't do what I told you, I'm going to teach all of the lesson myself tonight." "Elder, I've told you at least a thousand times . . . "

Nonverbal ways in which a bossy or punishing missionary communicates include deceiving, holding his head up haughtily and marching off angrily, being stubborn and/or disobedient, pointing his finger, shaking his fist, or pounding a table.

The Missionary Who Creates or Maintains Distance

Some missionaries engage in talk that fosters distance between themselves and their companions, making meaningful communication impossible. Such talk is often inconsistent with the subject being discussed, and may be impersonal, mechanical, keeping the discussion on a superficial plane. A missionary's communication with others may ignore the feelings of his companion or investigators. Sometimes a missionary will indulge in excess attempts at humor or evasiveness.

Such traits in one's speech may indicate to others that the missionary is aloof, superficial, noncaring, evasive, or noncommittal. This type of distance-creating communication is evidenced also by false starts, hesitant speech, or sentences that dwindle into incomplete statements.

The following dialogue demonstrates how Elder Jones maintains distance between himself and his companion, Elder Smith:

Elder Smith: You know, Elder Jones, I'm really sorry about tonight when you quoted that scripture and I jumped in and corrected you.

Elder Jones: Did we get any mail?

Smith: You turned red and I know you felt bad about it. I want to apologize.

Jones: What are we going to have for supper?   31

Smith: Well, you know I was wrong to do that.

Jones: Hey, we've got to clean up this mess in the living room before we turn in tonight.

Smith: Listen, I know you feel bad. Will you just accept my apology?

Jones: Let's just get this stuff cleaned up and turn in. I'm kind of tired.

Smith: Well, do you accept my apology? That was a bad thing for me to do.

Jones: Let's get this mess cleaned up and go to bed.

The Missionary Who Surrenders

When a missionary acquiesces, gives in, gives up, or apparently abandons his own beliefs and desires in deference to those of another person, his behavior indicates a fourth communication problem: surrendering. Often this type of behavior occurs when the companion is bossy and punishing and uses force and coercion with the missionary.

Surrendering should not be confused with the biblical injunction to turn the other cheek. (Matthew 5:39.) Rather, it is a strategy a frightened individual chooses to avoid responsibility in a relationship.

Many people surrender themselves to another person even when that person may not be using force of any kind. Some people have developed a lifestyle of continually giving in to the demands of others and of refusing to assert themselves. In our discussion of this communication problem, however, we will consider primarily the problem of giving in or surrendering as a result of the other person's use of force or pressure.

The following conversation illustrates a situation in which a missionary gives in to the demands of his companion even though he believes that what his companion is demanding is not right:

Elder Jones: Come on, Elder, I'm sweating like a goat. Let's go home.

Elder Smith: It's only four o'clock, Elder Jones. We should do a little more teaching before suppertime.

Jones: When you've been out for eighteen months like I have, you can count on one hand all the missionaries who stay out after four o'clock. We'll just take our time on the way home, and by the time we get back it ought to be time to eat. Maybe we can stop in at a few stores or something, talk to some people. That way no one will know we quit early. It's too hot to be doing much.

Smith: Well, I don't know.

Jones: Look, man, what are we going to do, sit out here and sweat?

Smith: Well, it is hot.

Jones: I haven't been this hot for a long time. We're not going to do any good this way. Everybody else quits early. Let's just head for home.

Smith: Oh, I don't know whether we should or not.

Jones: What are you—a straight guy or something? Let's just head for home.

Smith: Well, I guess we could stop by those stores on the way home.

Jones: Come on! It's hot out here. Let's go!

Smith: Alright.

A word of caution: As indicated in Doctrine and Covenants 121:43, there are times when we must

33

reprove "with sharpness, when moved upon by the Holy Ghost," and then show forth afterwards "an increase of love. . . ." Some of the behavior illustrated here could, in isolated situations, have a constructive impact and be considered righteous behavior. However, such behavior that is an ingrained habit will generally detract from a missionary's success in the mission field.

Becoming a True
Ambassador for Christ

*"And faith, hope, charity
and love, with an eye single to the
glory of God, qualify him
for the work."*—D&C 4:5

Babylon behavior—that which is ineffective or destructive—can be overcome if we have the courage to strive for more effective behavior to take its place. To symbolize this alternative type of behavior, we have chosen Zion, the great city of Enoch that has become a symbol of righteousness.

In Zion, each individual has an equal right to progress, unhindered by the Babylon behavior of others. Each person has an equal right to be viewed as a valuable, important son or daughter of our Heavenly Father.

Just as God has enough love for all of his children, the true missionary of Christ—the true missionary of The Church of Jesus Christ of Latter-day Saints—should be capable of loving all people.

The missionary who is Zion-like* is open and honest, respectful and considerate. He is cooperative, not competitive. He assumes responsibility for his own behavior and its possible influence on

*The following scriptures explain the characteristics of a Zion relationship: 2 Nephi 26:33; Mosiah 2:26; 4:13; 4:16-19; 23:7; Alma 16:16; 4 Nephi 2-3, 15-18; Moroni 7:44-48; D&C 4:5-6, 38:24-27, 51:9, 78:5-7, 82:17-20, 104:21, 121:41-45; Moses 7:18-19; Matthew 20:25-28; Acts 2:44-45, 4:32-35; 1 Corinthians 12:12-26; 2 Corinthians 8:14; Galatians 5:16, 5:22-26; James 1:27; 1 John 4:16, 18-21.

others. With limitless opportunity to progress as rapidly as he chooses, the Zion-like person measures his progress against his own performance or basic standards of excellence, not against those of others.

The missionary who communicates in a Zion-like manner is sincere, warm, friendly, approachable, openminded, and flexible. He is genuinely interested in others and has empathy for them. Demeaning, critical comments have no place in his relationships; if he feels change is needed, he negotiates for it respectfully and agreeably. His words, eyes, tone of voice, and body posture are harmonious with his inner spirit, his sense of self-worth, and his spirituality.

Those who come in contact with the Zion-like missionary—his companions, mission leaders, investigators, and others—feel his acceptance of them and of himself. Most of them instinctively trust him and feel a sense of belonging when they are with him, enhancing their own growth and development. The man of Babylon, however, usually feels uncomfortable and threatened by the Zion-like missionary.

Communication is the major consideration for the missionary who would be a man of Zion. He communicates with warmth, sincerity, empathy, and respect. He knows how to communicate well with others through the following means: (1) voicing his observations; (2) seeking to understand; (3) negotiating and committing; (4) encouraging; and (5) disclosing feelings. Let's review each of these areas to see if we can come to a better understanding of how they affect missionary work and relationships.

Voicing One's Observations

A person voices his observations when he reveals his ideas or thoughts; gives facts or opinions; answers questions; or tells of his observations concerning himself or another person or other persons, his relationship with the person to whom he is speaking, or his relationships with other people, events, and places. Rhetorical questions—questions that are asked merely for effect with no answer expected—are also verbal observations.

As he voices his observations, the Zion-like missionary speaks with a warm tone of voice, uses many statements with qualifiers, speaks in open-ended statements rather than closed ones, and indicates a willingness to share ideas and discussion time. Such characteristics make his communication experiences with others pleasant and even welcome. Among the phrases used by this type of missionary that encourage others and generate respect and warm feelings with his listeners are these:

"As I recall, it was yesterday . . ."

"I could be wrong, but I now think . . ."

"I think I can understand your needs better when . . ."

"It seems to me . . ."

"The Spirit of the Lord testifies to me that . . ."

These phrases are often followed by such questions as:

"How do you see it?"

"Is my perception close to yours?"

"Do you view this matter in a similar way?"

These questions are actually classified in the next category, however, and are thus listed here.

37

People who voice their observations in a caring way often use the word *feel* when they refer to what they think or believe. Their choice of words, particularly in the follow-up questions, indicates a willingness to share and to listen to the other person with an open mind.

Seeking to Understand

All questions, except those concerned with exploring alternatives or negotiating agreements, fit into the category of seeking to understand. This includes asking the other person for feedback, asking for his response to the accuracy of our perception, asking him to share his ideas, asking for permission, and asking for understanding or clarification of his ideas or feelings. Paraphrases in the form of questions or hypotheses (tentative assumptions) are also used by one who seeks to gain greater understanding. The following phrases indicate a desire for understanding:

"Let me see if I understand what you mean . . ."
"How do you feel when I . . .?"
"Please tell me why you get so upset with me when we . . ."
"Do I understand correctly? This is what I think you mean . . ."
"Do you believe that . . .?"

Qualifying phrases such as these, which route the message through the perception of the sender and imply consideration of the thoughts and feelings of the receiver, tend to make the communication experience acceptable and even welcome. It is, of course, important for the sender to give such messages in a spirit of warmth and friendliness.

Negotiating and Committing

Communication that consists of requests and/or questions that allow for discussion of various alternatives of action is characteristic of negotiating and committing. In this type of communication, the participants talk about or question the advantages and disadvantages of particular alternatives, negotiate for agreement, reach agreement, and commit themselves to decisions. If such discussion is Zion-like, it is carried out in an atmosphere of courtesy and respect, and any attempts to influence one another's decision are expressed in a friendly manner. Some phrases that facilitate this kind of discussion and atmosphere are:

"Please hand me my scriptures."
"Which of these methods do you feel is best?"
"Which alternative do you prefer?"
"I agree to . . . if you agree to . . ."

Questions about the mechanics of negotiating and reaching agreement also fit into this category, such as:

"How will we reach agreement on this?"
"Are we getting off the subject?"
"How can we change it so we both agree?"
"Do we agree to disagree?"

The nonverbal expressions of negotiating and committing must also be Zion-like. If the verbal communication appears Zion-like but the tone of voice or posture taken by one or both of the participants is Babylon-like, the communication is classified as being of Babylon.

39

Encouraging

Just as oil keeps machinery parts moving well with a minimum of friction, so encouragement freely given tends to increase the amount of communication and the satisfaction of the participants and to diminish friction.

Communication that is encouraging includes such expressions as "Mm-hmm," which indicates the listener is interested, supportive, and accepting. It includes identifying one's present feelings, prediction of future feelings, recollection of past feelings, apologies, paraphrases that take the form of declarations rather than questions, and empathic statements such as "I can see why you would feel frustrated and somewhat angry."

Encouraging interest and understanding can be expressed through statements such as the following:

"Please go on."

"As you practice teaching investigators, it will get easier for you."

"And so you became angry and upset."

"You're great!"

"You feel homesick now, but you'll learn to get over it."

The person we are trying to encourage will decide for himself whether our comments are encouraging, so it is important that we learn to "read" the responses of others. For example, if the other person slumps his shoulders and retreats from the task at hand, he probably does not feel encouraged. If, however, he throws his shoulders back and attacks the task with gusto, he more than likely feels encouraged.

Disclosing Feelings

Though the task of disclosing feelings may be difficult, it is necessary if communication is to function meaningfully. We disclose our feelings by bearing our testimony, telling others how we feel about ourself, about the other person, about our relationship with him, or about our relationship with Heavenly Father.

Our disclosure can consist of negative as well as positive feelings; however, if the negative feelings are expressed negatively, rather than in a courteous, respectful, positive manner, they can be classified as Babylon feelings. Examples of phrases that facilitate Zion-like interaction include the following:

"When you say that, I feel . . ."

"I feel hurt when . . ."

"I feel good when I think you appreciate . . ."

"I'm afraid to express my feelings to you when I think you might criticize me."

"The gospel of Christ has brought me great joy and happiness."

When we properly use each of the five types of Zion-like communication described above, we contribute to peace, harmony, and greater spirituality in our relationships with others. When we use a variety of these types of communication, in sensitive ways, our communication with others becomes far more interesting and effective.

In the dialogue that follows, two missionaries illustrate the use of Zion-like communication techniques to work themselves out of a Babylon relationship. The word or words in parentheses after each comment indicate the type of communication

41

being used; Babylon communication is expressed in tones of anger, while Zion communication is exhibited by warmth and friendliness.

Elder Smith: Elder Jones, I can't believe you took all the authority and arranged that meeting without asking me. It was a stupid move. You should have asked me first how to handle it. (*bossing or punishing*)

Elder Jones: I called and arranged that meeting so you wouldn't have to bother with it, and now you're ungrateful. (*punishing*)

Smith: What do you mean, ungrateful? Stick to the subject. We're talking about your doing something without my okay. It was a dumb thing to do. (*bossing and punishing*)

Jones: Look, Elder, you know you never take any responsibility. We should have had that meeting a week ago. But you were too lazy to arrange for it! (*punishing*)

Smith: Hey, let's slow down for a minute. What are we upset about? (*seeking to understand*)

Jones: I'm upset because you're so ungrateful and rude. I went out of my way to do your work and now you're upset. There's no pleasing you, is there! (*punishing*)

Smith: I'm upset because I feel it's my responsibility to call our contacts. I guess I'm feeling angry because I have put it off. (*disclosing feelings*) I'm sorry if I was ungrateful. (*encouraging*)

Jones: Well, I'm sorry too. (*encouraging*) But you see, I waited and waited for you to call the Nelsons so we could teach them, but you never did. (*voicing observation*)

Smith: You really think I'm not keeping up

with the appointments? (*seeking to understand*) I guess we haven't taught as much as we could. (*voicing observation*) I'll tell you what—if you'll help remind me, I'll try to become more responsible. (*negotiating and committing*)

Jones: That sounds great. (*encouraging*) How do you want me to remind you? (*negotiating*)

Smith: One thing you could do to help me would be to make sure I write down in our appointment book the names of those we are to call for teaching appointments. (*negotiating*) I believe the main reason I don't call is that I forget to write the names down in the first place. (*voicing observation*)

Jones: I'll do that. (*committing*) I'd be happy to. (*disclosing feelings*)

Thus we see that through using the Zion-like way of communication, wisely, sensitively, and righteously, the two missionaries harmoniously worked out of a Babylon situation, and each has taken a big step toward acquiring deeper spirituality and greater love for himself and his companion.

Making the Most
of Your Mission

"If thou wilt do good,
yea, and hold out faithful to the end,
thou shalt be saved
in the kingdom of God." —D&C 6:13

The speeding driver reads his speedometer, realizes he is going too fast, and slows his car down until the speedometer informs him he is within safe limits. He continues to monitor the speedometer in order to achieve his goal of keeping his vehicle's rate of travel within the legal limits.

The body builder uses his scales and tape measure to weigh and measure himself, and from this information he determines his present weight and body shape. Then he sets his goals. He continues to use the scales and tape measure to evaluate his progress from day to day in meeting his goals of decreasing or increasing his weight and developing his body.

A missionary can likewise measure his progress in retreating from Babylon relationships with his companions and others as he develops Zion interaction. In this chapter we present a means of measuring one's relationships that incorporates the concepts discussed in the previous chapters. By using this measuring device, a person can tell where he is in his communication, what he needs to do to have more righteous relationships, and his progress along the way. We also suggest six steps to help him learn how to use this device, or chart.

The knowledge and skills a missionary gains from learning to use the communication chart can aid him throughout his life. Not only can it help him improve relationships with companions, investigators, and leaders in the mission field, but it can also help him in his relationships with parents, friends, sweetheart, and, later on, his spouse and children. It can help him be a more effective leader in the Church, in his work, and in the community. Finally, and very importantly, it can help him talk more constructively with himself and thereby help him build a more positive self-image.

Step 1

Memorize the following nine categories with their corresponding numbers. They are the categories of communication discussed in the preceding chapters. Note that 1 through 5 are Zion styles of relating, while 6 through 9 are Babylon styles.

Zion Communication   *Babylon Communication*
1. Voicing observations   6. Soliciting attention
2. Seeking to understand 7. Bossing or punishing
3. Negotiating and com- 8. Creating or main-
   mitting   taining distance
4. Encouraging   9. Surrendering
5. Disclosing feelings

Step 2

Read and study the descriptions of each of the categories in Illustration 1, Communication Chart for Missionaries (CCM). Note that the chart includes ten categories; category 10, silence or confusion, is a new category we have not yet discussed. It is used when there is silence or when more than

Illustration 1 **Communication Chart for Missionaries (CCM)**

ZION COMMUNICATION

1. *Voicing observations*	Revealing ideas concerning oneself, the other person(s), the relationship, events or places; expressing observations; giving facts or opinions; asking rhetorical questions; answering the other person's questions; giving feedback
2. *Seeking to understand*	Asking questions; seeking to understand or to clarify; asking for response to accuracy of own perception; hypothesizing or guessing about meanings (may misunderstand, but is working respectfully to understand)
3. *Negotiating and committing*	Making requests; discussing or questioning alternatives; exploring or questioning their advantages or disadvantages; negotiating; agreeing; committing oneself to a decision (influencing by using respectful methods)
4. *Encouraging*	Praising; making encouraging statements; identifying; recalling and/or predicting the other person's feelings; accepting the other person's feelings; making empathic statements; paraphrasing the other person's feelings or thoughts
5. *Disclosing feelings*	Revealing one's own feelings concerning himself, the other person(s), the relationship, things, events, or places; disclosing negative feelings in a courteous manner

BABYLON COMMUNICATION

6. *Soliciting attention*	Monopolizing the conversation; interrupting; talking with little or no request for feedback; competing for

47

focus; drawing attention to oneself at the expense of the other person; bragging; parading oneself; seeking service or approval from others; seeking to please inappropriately; dropping names

7. *Bossing or punishing*

Bossing: lecturing; preaching; ordering; making intrusive statements; talking down to the other person(s); fighting to control; justifying oneself; talking angrily; whining; crying; complaining of being ill; using autocratic methods to control the other person(s). *Punishing:* belittling; demeaning; blaming; finding fault; using sarcasm; ridiculing

8. *Creating or maintaining distance*

Talking in an aloof, disinterested manner; wandering; talking continuously or off the subject; using humor that creates distance; ignoring feelings; intellectualizing; talking in a robot-like manner; agreeing automatically with little or no assertion of self; talking evasively; avoiding closeness

9. *Surrendering*

Giving in; abandoning one's own wants, wishes, and desires (often as a result of another person's Babylon behavior, as classified in category 7, above); giving up

MISCELLANEOUS

10. *Silence or confusion*

Keeping silent excessively; more than one person talking at a time

Adapted from G. Hugh Allred, *How to Strengthen Your Marriage and Family* (Provo, Utah: Brigham Young University Press, 1976.)

Research has shown that this chart can be used as a powerful and efficient vehicle to promote change in some relationships. (See T.G. Graff, "The effects of a structured communication program on female dyads in residence halls," unpublished doctoral dissertation, Brigham Young University, 1978.)

one person is talking at one time. Memorize the characteristics of this category also.

Step 3

In order to better understand how the chart can help you acquire knowledge and skill in communication, study the following dialogue between two missionaries. The numbers in parentheses* represent the categories of the chart and identify what type of communication is taking place.

After studying the dialogue, begin to systematically observe your own communication with others. Using the chart can help missionaries and all who wish to improve their communication with others by helping them to analyze problems in communication, determine what needs to be changed, and suggest ways in which changes can be made.

Elder Jones: Hey, Elder Smith, why don't you pick up your clothes and tuck in your shirt? (7)

Elder Smith: My clothes? (7) Look at your own clothes over in the corner. (7) This apartment has more of your things lying around than mine. (7)

Jones: I get so tired of seeing your things lying around. (7) I just give up. (7)

Smith: That's right—you just give up. (7) Just like today, always giving up. (7)

Jones: I don't either. (7) Hey, what are we doing? (2) What are we accomplishing, talking this way? (2)

Smith: We're just letting each other know where we stand. (7) We're looking at your clothes on the floor. (7)

*In determining which number to select, when in doubt choose the higher one for example, select 5 over 3.

Jones: I think there must be a better way to get at this. (3) We're out here to do the Lord's work. (1) There must be a better way to get along. (3) I'm sorry. (4) I really ought to pick up my things. (4)

Smith: You really mean that? (2)

Jones: Yes, I'll try to keep the apartment neater. (3) I feel a lot better when I return if the place is clean. (5) It makes me feel better about the work and everything else. (5)

Smith: You're just saying that because we had a bad day outside today. (7) If we'd had a good day, you'd still throw your clothes down on the floor. (7)

Jones: Not really. (1) What do you think? (2) Don't you prefer coming home to a clean apartment? (2)

Smith: Sure. I have to admit that I feel better when it is clean. (5) But I just wonder if you're going to pick up your clothes. (7)

Jones: Well, there's no problem there. (1) I'll be glad to pick them up. (3) It's hard for me to get motivated sometimes, and it's discouraging to come home to a dirty apartment. (5) I'd like to see us both make it a point to clean up before we leave in the morning. (3) What do you think about that? (3)

Smith: I think I would feel better if we could clean up before we left. (5) If the place is clean and I knew I'd be coming home to a clean place, I'd probably even feel better about doing the work. (5)

Jones: You don't feel like I'm being hard on you for leaving a mess around here, do you? (2) I realize I'm just as much to blame as you are. (4)

Smith: I did at first, when you started talking. (1) But I guess we probably both need to realize that we've had a bad day. (4) No one let us in and we got a few doors slammed in our faces. (1) It's pretty hard to come home and be decent to each other after that kind of day, (5) but we probably ought to watch that too. (3)

Jones: Yes. (3) What you're saying, then, is that when things go bad, we should be careful about how we interact with each other. (4)

Smith: That's for sure. (4)

Jones: We got off to a bad start there, right? (2)

Smith: Yes. (4) I appreciate your understanding on that. (4) If you'll watch it, I'll watch it too, (3) and we can probably get a lot closer together. (4)

Jones: I really feel good about the way things are working out. (5) It makes me feel as if I'm doing something right. (5)

Smith: I think you're right. (4) You know, the big problem with me is that my pride gets in the way, (1) and then I hate to say I'm sorry or to admit I'm wrong. (5)

Jones: I feel that way too. (5)

Smith: Why don't we—I mean, we could do one of two things: we could pick up our things right now and eat later, or we could eat now and then stay up a little later tonight to clean up. (3) What do you think? (3)

Jones: Let's go ahead and eat now and then clean up later. (3)

Smith: Okay, let's. (3)

Step 4

Now memorize two or three of the phrases from each of the categories in the Zion-relationship style. They are repeated here for your convenience. Memorizing these phrases will help you draw on

51

them as you work to improve your communication. Practice using phrases from a variety of Zion categories, to enrich your communication and make it more interesting as well as more helpful.

Voicing one's observations:
"As I recall, it was yesterday . . ."
"I could be wrong, but I now think . . ."
"I think I can understand your needs better when . . ."
"It seems to me . . ."
"The Spirit of the Lord testifies to me that . . ."

Seeking to understand:
"Let me see if I understand what you mean . . ."
"How do you feel when I . . . ?"
"Please tell me why you get so upset with me when we . . ."
"Do I understand correctly? This is what I think you mean . . ."
"Do you believe that . . . ?"

Negotiating and committing:
"Please hand me my scriptures."
"Which of these methods do you feel is best?"
"What do you see as possible courses of action available to us?"
"Which alternative do you prefer?"
"I agree to . . . if you agree to . . ."
"How will we reach agreement on this?"
"Are we getting off the subject?"
"How can we change it so we both agree?"
"Do we agree to disagree?"

Encouraging:
"Please go on."
"As you practice teaching investigators, it will become easier for you."

"And so you became angry and upset."

"You're great!"

"You feel homesick now, but you'll learn to get over it."

Disclosing feelings:

"When you say that, I feel . . ."

"I feel hurt when . . ."

"I feel good when I think you appreciate . . ."

"I'm afraid to express my feelings to you when I think you might criticize me."

"The gospel of Christ has brought me great joy and happiness."

Step 5

One way to measure communication with others is to mentally classify it, or, even better, to use tally sheets such as in Illustration 2, to identify various patterns of communication. This might be done by recording on cassette tapes conversations with missionary companions and/or investigators and then playing them back when it is convenient. Record the conversation on the tally sheets by (1) categorizing phrases and sentences according to the descriptions on the communication chart for missionaries and (2) marking down how many times each type of communication (Zion or Babylon) occurs.

Illustration 2 is a completed tally sheet of the dialogue between Elder Jones and Elder Smith under Step 3. It shows that both communicated in category 7 (bossing or punishing), and also the amount each communicated in this style. It further indicates that Elder Smith could have reached out more to Elder Jones by making more responses in category 2 (seeking to understand).

53

Illustration 2   **Tally Sheet**

CATEGORIES	PERSON A (Elder Jones)	PERSON B (Elder Smith)
1. Voicing observations	///	///
2. Seeking to understand	⊥H⊤ /	/
3. Negotiating or committing	⊥H⊤ ///	⊥H⊤
4. Encouraging	////	⊥H⊤ /
5. Disclosing feelings	⊥H⊤ /	⊥H⊤
6. Soliciting attention		
7. Bossing or punishing	////	⊥H⊤ ⊥H⊤
8. Creating or maintaining distance		
9. Surrendering		
MISCELLANEOUS 10. Silence or confusion		

ZION COMMUNICATION (categories 1–5)

BABYLON COMMUNICATION (categories 6–9)

54

Use tally sheets like this one for recording your own conversations to determine where you need to improve and the progress you are making in reaching your goals.

Step 6

Now that you have memorized each category of the chart by name and number, have a clear understanding of its definition, and know how to measure your communication using this chart, you are in a good position to work systematically to improve your relationship with others.

Since trying to do too much at any one time may lead to discouragement, you might prefer to work at improving in only one category for a given period of time. For example, suppose you find that you communicate far too much in category 7 (bossing or punishing) and too little in categories 4 (encouraging) and 5 (disclosing feelings). You are convinced that by stopping your inappropriate communication in category 7 and increasing and improving your communication in categories 4 and 5 you can demonstrate greater love and concern for others and thereby strengthen your missionary efforts. But you feel somewhat confused about how to manage what you need to do. How might you proceed?

One effective approach might be to divide your efforts into blocks of two or three days, and emphasize improvement in only one category each day. For example, your schedule might read as follows:

Day	Goal
1	I will effectively encourage my companion (category 4) at least five times today.

55

2   I will effectively disclose my feelings (category 5) at least five times today.

3   I will not unrighteously use bossing or punishing behavior (category 7) on anyone today.

At the end of the third day, begin the cycle again. When you are concentrating on one category, work on others at the same time if you can use them easily and appropriately. Your efforts to improve and measure your progress would, however, generally be better served by concentrating on only one category at a time. Revise your schedule as you reach specific goals and new learning becomes easy and habitual, and as you discover other areas you feel you need to work on.

Caution, Courage, and Success

Attempting to improve communication with another person is more effective when both participants are sincere in their efforts to improve. When one has a set pattern of using Babylon communication and is not interested in changing, the other person must make greater effort to effect changes. The models of Zion and Babylon communication are abstractions that should be applied to reality with sensitivity and common sense.

Babylon behavior as a general lifestyle is basically unhealthy, nonconstructive, and at times even destructive. The same is not true of all Babylon-type communication, however. Speaking sharply (category 7), when inspired by the Holy Ghost, to a companion who is slothful in his work (see D&C 121:43) or surrendering (category 9) to the assertions of a companion who is learning to

56

assert himself could both be constructive behaviors. A companion who is used to surrendering himself to the unrighteous demands of others (category 9) and who is working to change this behavior may find himself lashing out at others (category 7) as he begins to change. In such a situation, moving from passively surrendering to actively asserting can indicate real progress and may be necessary before he can become skillful in expressing himself in a Christlike manner.

What we are suggesting is that Babylon-type communication may be necessary in isolated situations or as a transition from poor to better communication. It is important, however, that the individuals involved evaluate any Babylon-like responses within the total context of the interaction to determine if such responses are constructive and growth-producing. When Babylon communication is used as a necessary part of a given relationship it must be done with great sensitivity, a deep understanding of its probable impact on the other person, and the witness of the Holy Ghost that it is to be used. The possibilities of Babylon communication having constructive influence are minimal under the following conditions:

1. When it is used habitually and frequently—sure evidence of a Babylon lifestyle.

2. When the person responding with Babylon behavior is unaware that he is doing so.

3. When the person is aware of his behavior but does not have a sound rationale and/or inspiration for it.

4. When he has not developed skill in Zion ways of communicating.

57

5. When he generally believes that his own self-worth is tied to his use of Babylon responses. He may think that to be worthwhile, he has to keep the attention of others focused on him, have power over them, make them suffer, keep his distance from them, or give in to their demands.

At first the missionary who is trying to change from a Babylon style of communication to Zion behavior may feel frustrated, and he may wonder if the changes are really worth the frustration and time involved. But as he becomes increasingly accustomed to communicating with others more effectively, he will notice changes taking place. He will find it easier to talk with others and to develop deep friendships with them. Life will take on an entirely new meaning for him as others respond to his behavior by relating to him with greater respect, love, and trust. His earnest, courageous, and prayerful efforts to change will be rewarded with a greater sense of peace and spirituality.

In the mission field each person has a tremendous opportunity—and responsibility—to increase his righteous behavior, setting a model for spirituality as he influences those with whom he comes in contact. He thereby becomes a true ambassador for Christ in spreading happiness, joy, and peace.

It is our prayer that each one will achieve his goal of a successful mission and find the inner tranquillity and joy with himself and our Heavenly Father that such an accomplishment ensures.

Allred, G. Hugh. *How to Strengthen Your Marriage and Family.* Provo, Utah: Brigham Young University Press, 1976.

Allred, G. Hugh. *The Challenge to Be One.* Provo, Utah: Brigham Young University Press, 1974.

Nibley, Hugh. "What Is Zion: A Distant View." *Joseph Smith Lecture Series.* Provo, Utah: ASBYU Academics, 1972-73.

Pratt, Orson. *New Jerusalem and Equality and Oneness of the Saints.* Salt Lake City: Parker P. Robison.

Sicher, Lydia. "Education for Freedom." *The Journal of Individual Psychology,* 11 (2).

Acknowledgments

We express heartfelt appreciation to our wives, Carolyn and Nani, for their sensitive and valuable critiques of the manuscript.

We are grateful to John Plaisted, who assisted in the dialogues; to Kerril Sue Rollins, who helped edit the manuscript; and to Marilyn Jensen and others in the Department of Child Development and Family Relationships at Brigham Young University, who typed the manuscript.

We express thanks also to Alfred Adler for his ideas concerning birth order and psychological position in the family, and to Rudolph Dreikurs and Lydia Sicher, who articulated along with G. Hugh Allred the Adlerian concepts of vertical and level relationships. These psychological models of relationships support the Babylon and Zion models that are so important to this book. Ideas from communication theorists, including Ned A. Flanders, Edmund J. Amidon, and Paul Watzlawic, contribute much to the text.

We express heartfelt thanks to Lowell M. Durham, Jr., director of publishing at Deseret Book, for his faith in the manuscript, and to members of his staff who helped in the editing, design, production and publication of it.

Adaptations are reprinted by permission of Brigham Young University Press from G. Hugh Allred, *How to Strengthen Your Marriage and Family* (Brigham Young University Press, copyright 1976), chapters 2, 3, and 11. We thank BYU Press for this courtesy. You may wish to read the above book to see how the ideas presented here are applied to family life.

Tally Sheet

CATEGORIES	PERSON A	PERSON B
1. Voicing observations		
2. Seeking to understand		
3. Negotiating or committing		
4. Encouraging		
5. Disclosing feelings		
6. Soliciting attention		
7. Bossing or punishing		
8. Creating or maintaining distance		
9. Surrendering		
MISCELLANEOUS 10. Silence or confusion		

ZION COMMUNICATION (categories 1–5)

BABYLON COMMUNICATION (categories 6–9)

Tally Sheet

	CATEGORIES	PERSON A	PERSON B
ZION COMMUNICATION	1. Voicing observations		
	2. Seeking to understand		
	3. Negotiating or committing		
	4. Encouraging		
	5. Disclosing feelings		
BABYLON COMMUNICATION	6. Soliciting attention		
	7. Bossing or punishing		
	8. Creating or maintaining distance		
	9. Surrendering		
	MISCELLANEOUS 10. Silence or confusion		

Tally Sheet

CATEGORIES	PERSON A	PERSON B
ZION COMMUNICATION 1. Voicing observations		
2. Seeking to understand		
3. Negotiating or committing		
4. Encouraging		
5. Disclosing feelings		
BABYLON COMMUNICATION 6. Soliciting attention		
7. Bossing or punishing		
8. Creating or maintaining distance		
9. Surrendering		
MISCELLANEOUS 10. Silence or confusion		

Tally Sheet

CATEGORIES	PERSON A	PERSON B
ZION COMMUNICATION 1. Voicing observations		
2. Seeking to understand		
3. Negotiating or committing		
4. Encouraging		
5. Disclosing feelings		
BABYLON COMMUNICATION 6. Soliciting attention		
7. Bossing or punishing		
8. Creating or maintaining distance		
9. Surrendering		
MISCELLANEOUS 10. Silence or confusion		

About the Authors

Dr. G. Hugh Allred is a professor at Brigham Young University, where he trains marriage and family counselors. He is a Fellow and Approved Supervisor of marriage and family counselors with the American Association of Marriage and Family Counselors and chairman of the advisory committee to the Governor of Utah for the licensing of marriage and family counselors. Dr. Allred's church service has included membership in a bishopric, many ward and stake leadership and teaching positions, and membership on church writing committees. He is the author of many articles and books, including *How to Strengthen Your Marriage and Family* and *Mission for Mother.*

Steve H. Allred served in the Georgia-South Carolina Mission as a district leader, zone leader, and public relations director. He is presently the in-service leader for the teachers of adult Sunday School classes in his ward. He works at the Utah State Training School for the Mentally Retarded, and is also attending Brigham Young University, where he is working toward a degree in child development and family relationships.